Ultimate FACTIVITY Co

ANGRY BIRDS STAR WARS™

Contents

This book belongs to: ____________________

Chapter 1

Brave Birds

A group of angry but heroic birds are in a deadly battle with the Pig Empire. This feathered flock must find the mysterious Egg, which contains the Force. If the greedy porkers get their trotters on it, they will use it to rule the galaxy.

Chuck "Ham" Solo

Chuck "Ham" Solo got his nickname from smuggling junk food across the galaxy. Before meeting the Rebel Birds, he spent his days gambling and doing his own thing. He hates being told what to do!

Yoda Bird

Yoda Bird is a powerful Jedi. He is as wise as an owl and shares the secrets of the Force with eager young Jedi Birds. The only thing he will not reveal is the truth about The Egg.

Red Skywalker

Red Skywalker may be young, but he is eager to leave the nest and join the Rebel Birds. This blundering bird is very brave, but he can be clumsy – he is always dropping his lightsaber!

Stella Organa

Princess Stella Organa is one of the leaders of a flock of Rebel Birds called the Bird Republic. This fiesty bird likes being in charge, and she can be a bit of a drama queen when things don't go her way.

Moa Windu

This talented Jedi Bird is often very suspicious and grumpy – he always has a frown on his face. If Moa thinks that someone could be a threat to the Jedi Bird Order, he will watch them like a hawk.

Lando Birdissian

Lando Birdissian is a feathered friend of Chuck's. His charm and his talent for gambling has made him a very rich bird. The Rebel Birds know they need a quick-thinking bird like him on their side.

R2-EGG2

This helpful astromech droid bird is always willing to lend a wing to the Rebel Birds. What they don't know is that The Egg is hidden inside him – Yoda Bird put it there without telling anyone!

Obi-Wan Kaboomi

Obi-Wan Kaboomi is a great Jedi Knight – but he can't always control his explosions! He spent many years disguised as an ordinary bird, but now he is ready to join the fight against the Pig Empire.

Jedi Bird Warriors

Spot the Jedi Birds

The brave Jedi Birds flock together to stop the pigs from taking over the galaxy. The Jedi Birds are trained in the Force and to avoid the temptations of the Pork Side. But no Jedi Bird is the same as another...

Read about the Jedi Birds, then use the clues to identify each bird.

Quail-Gon

Quail-Gon is probably the angriest bird of all. He often strays from the flock to do things his own way.

Yoda Bird

Jedi Bird Master Yoda is the wise and respected leader of the Jedi Birds. He is really old, but Yoda is no birdbrain.

Obi-Wan Kaboomi

Obi-Wan is an excellent teacher. Just don't get on the wrong side of him – he has an explosive temper!

Redkin Skywalker

Young Redkin is fearless, impatient, and a skilled Podracing pilot. He loves building machines.

I have a large beak.

↓

I have dark brown feathers.

↓

I like to do things my way.

↓

1 My name is:

____

____

Find our **stickers** at the back of the book.

I have a short temper.

I wear brown.

I am a great teacher.

2 My name is:

I have no fear.

I have spiky hair.

I hate waiting for things.

3 My name is:

I have a lightsaber.

I am a wise leader.

I have wrinkles on my forehead.

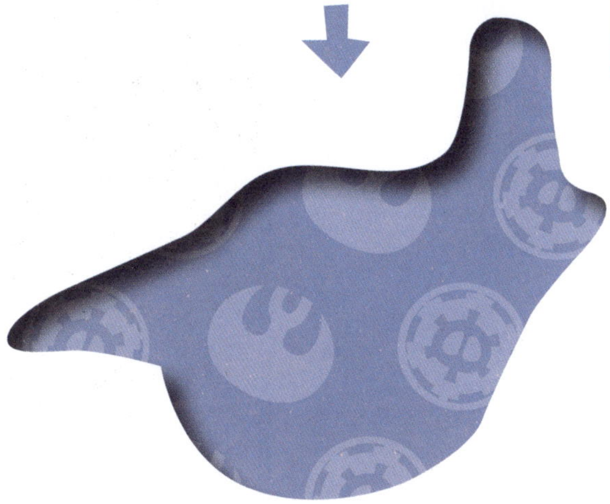

4 My name is:

Find the **answers** on page 97.

Rebel Bird Style

Draw your own Rebel Bird

Read about the Rebel Birds' different looks to help you design your own.

The Rebel Birds come in all sorts of shapes and sizes. Whether it's a Jedi Bird, a smuggler or a princess, each bird has its own unique look.

Obi-Wan Kaboomi

Obi-Wan wears a big brown **cloak**, which helps him stay hidden from evil Pigs.

Red Skywalker

Eager young Red wears a **belt**, so he can carry anything handy. He keeps his lightsaber by his side and is always ready for action!

Lando Birdissian

Lando always wears a **stylish** outfit and keeps his moustache neatly groomed. Looking good makes it easier to impress other birds!

Princess Stella

Stella knows that having unique **hair** always gets you noticed – perfect for a Bird Rebel Princess!

Setting a trend

Whether it's a cool accessory, crazy hair or a neat little gadget, Rebel Birds like to have something that sets them apart from the rest.

What sort of **hair** will your bird have?

Will your bird wear a **hat**?

Does your bird need a **weapon**?

Your bird's feathers and **outfit** can be any **colour** you like!

My bird's name is: ____________________

Sneaky Smuggler

Complete the checklist

Charming but cocky Chuck "Ham" Solo is a famous junk food smuggler. He often has no idea what he's doing, but he thinks that he is one cool bird. He is sure that he has what it takes to be the best smuggler in the galaxy.

Ham the Hero

Chuck's bravery makes him one of the best birds to have on your side. Despite mixing with some shifty criminals, he often lends a wing to help the Bird Rebels.

Read about what you need to be a smuggler and choose the stickers to complete the checklist.

Weapon

I don't like lightsabers, but I always keep a weapon by my side. You never know who might be on your tail!

Smart friend

My smooth-squawking buddy can fool anybody. He has gotten us out of a few sticky spots!

Spaceship

My ship is always ready for a speedy getaway across the galaxy.

Ready for action

Smuggers aren't everyone's favourite bird, so we must always be prepared for battle.

Sidekick

Every smuggler needs a sidekick – mine is a fearsome fuzzball!

Chuck's checklist

1. My powerful blaster.

☐

2. My smart friend, Lando Birdissian.

☐

3. My amazing spaceship, *The Mighty Falcon.*

☐

4. My sidekick, Terrebacca.

☐

5. I must be ready for battle!

☐

Put a **tick** in each box once you find the stickers.

Find the **stickers** at the back of the book.

The Rebel Birds

Complete the recruitment poster

Read about what it takes to be a good Rebel Bird, then complete the poster.

The Rebel Birds aren't about to let a bunch of greedy swine tell them what to do! This band of feathered heroes is fighting back against the evil pigs. They will stop at nothing to halt Lard Vader in his trottered tracks.

Brave

Young fowl Red Skywalker is a proud member of the Rebel Birds and the bravest pilot in their ranks. He can whizz across the galaxy, outrunning much bigger spaceships.

Team player

Terebacca is fiercely loyal to his best bud, Chuck Solo. He knows that when Rebel Birds work together as a team, the podgy pigs had better watch out!

Smart

The Rebels are just a few small birds fighting against a very powerful Pig Empire. Chuck Solo has to come up with cunning and crafty plans for the rebels to avoid being destroyed by their dangerous pork enemy.

Great leader

Princess Stella Organa is a strong leader! She isn't afraid to be bossy, and she makes sure everyone obeys her orders immediately – that's how things get done!

Colour in the picture on the poster.

Do you want the chance to show your skills?

THE REBEL BIRDS NEED YOU!

To join the Rebel Birds you will need to be:

Write what you think a new Rebel Bird should be.

The Pig Star

Get through the maze to escape

The Rebel Birds have been captured and taken to the Pig Star – the largest pig-made battle station in the galaxy! They must find a way to escape before the pigs catch them.

Pigtrooper

Pigtroopers are Lard Vader's soldiers. They are loyal but not too clever. Make a noise and run about, then slip past as they try to figure out what is going on.

Make your way through the maze, battling the villains as you go. Add a sticker for every victory.

The Pig Star

The Pig Star even looks like a pig – it has a huge snout and piggy ears! This vast vessel can zap an entire planet into stardust.

Lard Vader

Yikes – you are face to face with Lard Vader! He thinks the Rebel Birds have The Egg and will not let them escape. Prepare for the lightsaber duel of your life!

Pig Star trooper II

Troopers rely on junk food from the Pig Star's canteen to keep them going. Once they start eating, not much distracts them. You can tiptoe right on past.

Pig Star trooper I

Pig Star troopers are Pork Side soldiers who run the Pig Star and operate its deadly weapons. To defeat them, you must dodge their laser blasters. Be quick!

FINISH

Congratulations!

You've escaped the Pig Star! You can now head to a safe planet where C-3PYOLK and R2-EGG2 are waiting for you.

Bird Blog

Write Redkin Skywalker's blog posts

Read about Redkin's journey as a Jedi Bird, then write his blog posts about his feelings.

Young Redkin Skywalker is training to be a Jedi Master. He has more Force power than any other bird – but he often loses his temper. He also can't resist eating too much junk food. Will this determined bird fight for the Jedi, or will his impatient ways lead him to the Pork Side?

A flying start

Young Redkin was spotted by Jedi Bird Quail-Gon Jinn. Quail-Gon believed that this chick was the Chosen One and could save the galaxy from the evil pigs.

Jedi Birds

Obi-Wan Kaboomi takes Redkin under his wing, and they become best bird buddies. Redkin is really **happy**. But Redkin finds it harder to get along with Moa Windu – Moa doesn't trust him!

Young lovebirds

Redkin has a crush on Peckmé – he is so **nervous** he can barely even open his beak when she's around! The only thing he loves more than spending time with her is snacking on tasty junk food.

Temptation

As time goes by, Redkin becomes **confused and angry**. He is sure the Jedi Birds are keeping secrets about the mysterious Egg. Could the evil pig Darth Swindle have the answers?

Redkin's Blog

Redkin Skywalker

Location: Coruscant

Status: Happy!

Obi-Wan Kaboomi likes this

Redkin Skywalker

Location: Naboo

Status: Nervous!

Peckmé Amidala likes this

Redkin Skywalker

Location: Coruscant

Status: Angry!

Darth Swindle likes this

About me

*My name is Redkin Skywalker. I am a Jedi Bird Knight.
My hobbies include Podracing and building cool droids.
My favourite food is anything with chips!*

Fact Challenge

How does Redkin feel about **Obi-Wan**?

How does Redkin feel around **Peckmé**?

What makes Redkin **lose his temper**?

Factivity Challenge

Test your knowledge on Chapter 1

Answer each question. If you need help, look back through the section.

Now that you have finished the first chapter of the book, take the Factivity Challenge to find out if you can defeat the Pork Side!

1. Find the sticker that best matches the description:

This sidekick is a fearsome fuzzball.

2. Which two of these are Jedi Birds?

Yoda Bird ☐ **Obi-Wan Kaboomi** ☐ **R2-EGG2** ☐

3. Lando Birdissian wears a green cape.

True ☐ **False** ☐

4. Who is this Bird? ____________________

____

5. Redkin Skywalker is tempted to the Pork Side by Darth ____________________.

Find the **answers** on page 97.

Now that you have finished the Challenge, fill this scene with your extra stickers!

Chapter 2

Pig Villains

The Pig Empire is led by scary Sith Lards. These podgy porkers are always trying to sniff out The Egg, only stopping to stuff their faces with as much junk food as possible. They are hungry for power and will not let bothersome birds stand in their way.

Lard Vader

Lard Vader may be on the side of the pigs, but he was once a Jedi Bird. His hunger for junk food and power lured him to the Pork Side. Now he works for Darth Swindle and leads the piggy army.

Darth Swindle

This sneaky swine once pretended to be respectable Emperor Piglatine. As the evil leader of the Pig Empire, he bans junk food all across the galaxy – so he can eat it all himself!

Jabba the Hog

Jabba the Hog is a greedy crime boss. He works behind Lard Vader's back, buying, selling and eating junk food. This slimy smuggler has no problem with turning his enemies into tasty snacks!

Find the **stickers** at the back of the book.

Count Dodo

Count Dodo may look like a gentle old pig, but beneath the long cloak and neatly trimmed beard lies a hateful hog. This proud porker was once a Jedi, but his love of sweets led him to the Pork Side.

Darth Moar

Count Dodo's apprentice, Darth Moar, is one seriously scary pig! This crazy Sith enjoys fighting Jedi Birds even more than eating junk food! They had better beware of his double-bladed lightsaber.

Pigtrooper

Pigtroopers have no ideas of their own. The Sith Lards have trained these soldiers to follow orders without question. They blunder around the galaxy, searching for junk food to bring back to Darth Swindle.

General Grunter

General Grunter is a cyborg warrior who works for the pigs, but underneath his mask lies a scaly reptile! While he may be scary, his nasty cough makes it impossible for him to sneak up on anyone.

The Pork Side

Identify the Pig Villains

The pigs from the Pork Side are hungry for two things – junk food and power! Here are some of the peskiest and most persistent pig villains to ever take on the brave Bird Rebels.

Identify the villain in each zoomed-in picture.

Read about the villains and find their stickers at the back of the book.

The Bird Rebels may be attacked by the pigs at any time!

Lard Vader

The power-hungry leader of the pig army wears a sinister **helmet** with **red eyepieces**. Its built-in **mask** helps him breathe, but makes his breathing really noisy.

Jabba the Hog

Jabba is a greedy, **yellow-eyed** crime boss who loves to buy, sell, and eat junk food. Jabba's **flabby body** has no skeleton, and his skin oozes a smelly slime that can be used for cooking.

Darth Swindle

This mysterious leader of the Pig Empire is an expert in using Sith lightning. He hides his identity by wearing a **cloak**. The only bit of him that can be seen poking out is his **snout**.

Darth Moar

This dangerous Sith apprentice has **red and black tattoos** that show he comes from the Nightboar tribe of Dathomir. Sharp **horns** grow around the top of his head.

Count Dodo

Once a wise Jedi, Count Dooku was lured to the Pork Side with the promise of snacks. This deadly duellist keeps his **white beard** combed and his silver **cloak clasp** polished.

General Grunter

Cyborg General Grunter is not really a pig – he is a reptile. His cold, **reptilian eyes** give him away! General Grunter was blown up years ago, and Count Dodo rebuilt him as a pig, complete with a **metal snout**.

1 Bearded bad guy

2 Tribal horns

3 Part reptile, part machine

4 Crime and slime

5 Under the hood

6 Helmeted leader

Find the **answers** on page 97.

Scary Sith

Design your own Sith Pig

The ancient Sith enemy of the Jedi Birds are the craziest and scariest pigs in the galaxy. No two Sith Pigs look alike – but they are all as frighteningly ugly as each other!

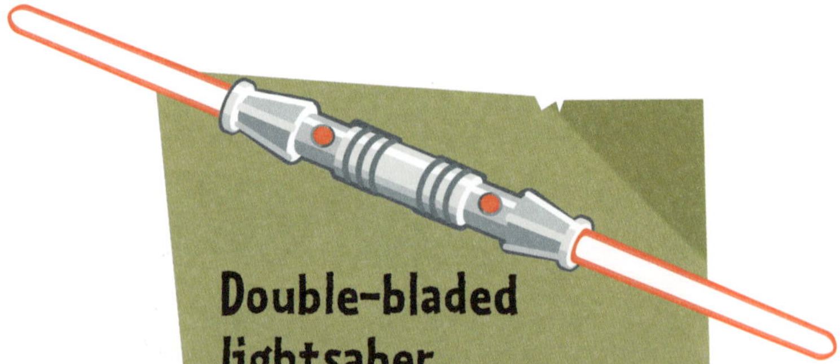

Double-bladed lightsaber

Darth Moar's weapon of choice has two deadly blades so that it can do twice as much damage!

Read all about Darth Moar, then design your own Sith Pig.

Darth Moar

Darth Moar is one of the fiercest-looking Sith Pigs around. His scary red and black facial tattoos have most birds running for cover.

Freaky faces

Don't by fooled by this sneaky swine's smile. Dangerous Darth Moar is really planning his next attack!

Can't you just see the hunger for power in his eyes? Moar will stop at nothing to get his porky way.

Now something has really made Moar mad! Quick! Feed him some junk food. That might calm him down.

You can clearly see the Pork Side in Moar's twisted, angry face. It is definitely time to take a step back...!

What sort of **horns** will your Sith Pig have?

What **colour** will your Sith Pig be?

Will your Sith Pig have **tattoos?**

Will your Sith Pig have a **lightsaber**?

Will your Sith Pig be **angry** or **smiling**?

Swindle in Command

Complete the sticker jigsaw

Behind every evil scheme in the galaxy lurks the hooded snout of Darth Swindle. Sith Pigs, Pigtroopers, battle pigs and bounty hunters all stand ready to follow this swine's wicked orders.

Read about the things that appear in the jigsaw, then use the sticker pieces to put it together.

Darth Swindle

Darth Swindle is the evil leader of the Pig Empire. This hooded villain is both dangerous and mysterious. Who knows what dastardly plans he is dreaming up?

Battle pig

Battle pigs are the robotic foot soldiers of the Pork Side. What they lack in brains they make up for in sheer numbers.

Jango Fatt

Jango Fatt is a greedy bounty hunter. Darth Swindle has offered to pay him his weight in junk food if he can catch Obi-Wan and Quail-Gon.

Escape the Pork Side!

Caught in one of Darth Swindle's villainous traps, Obi-Wan and Quail-Gon have to escape from a Pork Side battleship! One more hit and they're done for!

Find the **stickers** at the back of the book.

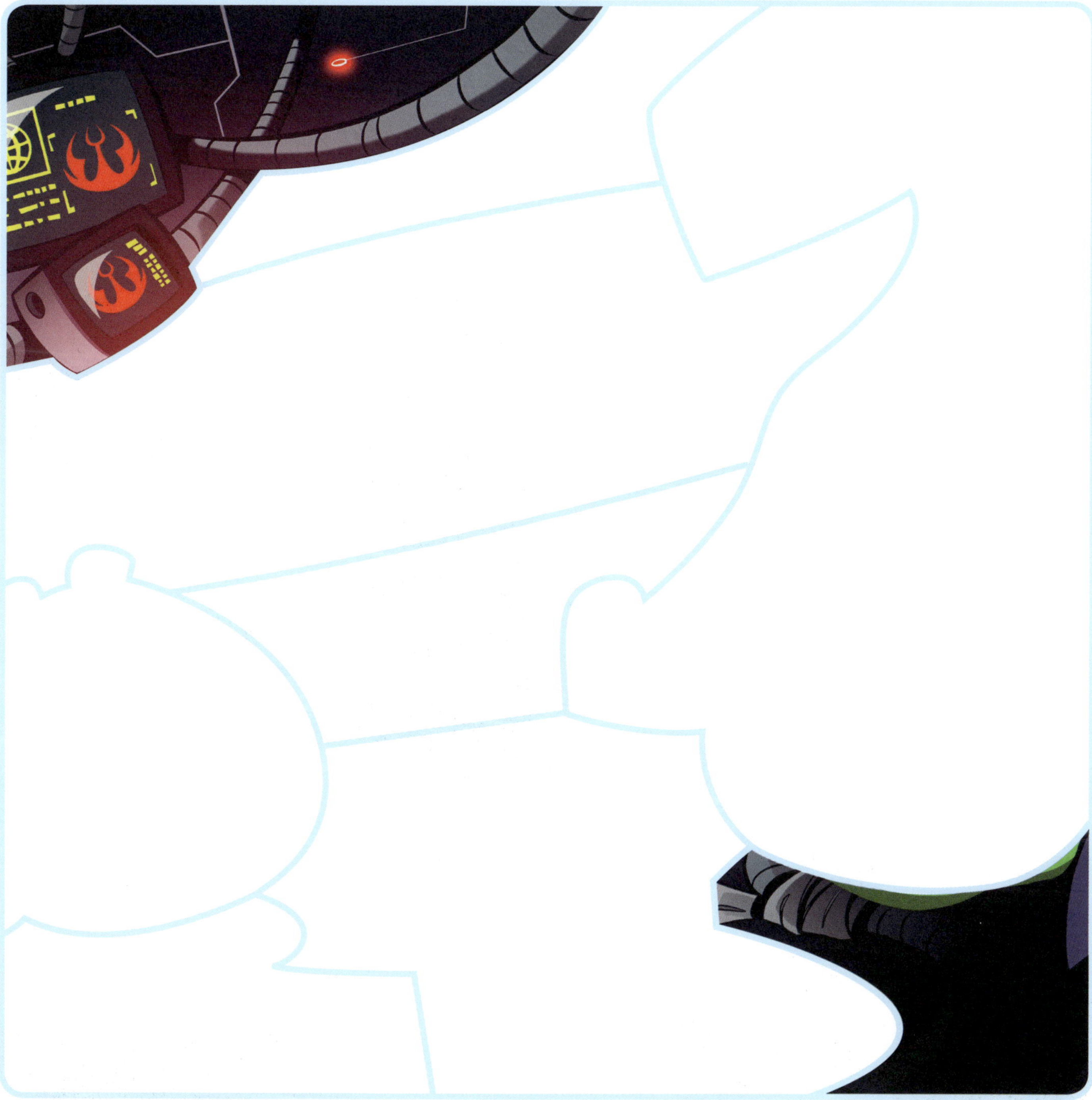

Describe what you think is happening here.

Lard Vader

Draw the Pig Star troopers

Read about Lard Vader then draw the Pig Star troopers that hide under his cloak.

Evil Lard Vader loves trying to ruffle the Rebel Birds' feathers. Whenever he wants to appear extra scary, he finds the nearest two Pig Star troopers and sits on top of them. This makes him look like the tallest pig in the galaxy!

On the Pig Star

Lard Vader grills Princess Stella for information about The Egg. He may look tall, but he is very short-tempered, so he is furious when Stella keeps her beak shut.

Dinnertime

Lard Vader crashes a Cloud City dinner party! The bird bully towers over the Rebel Birds, as bounty hunter Boba Fatt arrests them.

Epic duel

When it comes to lightsaber duelling, Lard Vader doesn't fight fairly. Eating too much junk food means that he is not as fit as he used to be, so he stands on his piggy minions and lets them do the work.

Pig Star trooper

There isn't much going on inside a Pig Star trooper's head, but the outside is comfortable and round – perfect for sitting on!

Don't forget to draw the pigs' **helmets**.

Colour your pigs in **green**.

Dodo's Droids

Spot the droids

The armies of the Pork Side are full of dastardly droids, because only robots are stupid enough to follow pig orders. Evil Count Dodo has designed lots of different mechanical menaces for different jobs.

Count Dodo

This fancy pig thinks he is superior to everyone, even Darth Swindle. His pig pals are all robots – no one else can stand him!

Read about the droids, then use the clues to identify each droid.

General Grunter

This Pork Side general isn't really a droid. He was blown apart a long time ago, but Count Dodo collected all the pieces and rebuilt him!

Imperial probe droid

Probe droids are sneaky, shadowy pests. They hunt for Rebel Bird bases and then send pictures back for the Pig Empire to chew on.

Battle pig

Real pigs aren't that clever, but these robotic ones make them look like geniuses. Ducking, dodging or taking cover is too complicated for these dummies.

Warhog

Warhogs are deadly enemies. They carry an arsenal of weapons and can change shape! Jedi Birds need to be careful around these metal monsters.

I have metal skin.

I have yellow eyes.

Count Dodo put me back together.

1 I am: ______________________

Find our **stickers** at the back of the book.

I have ears.

I was built for battle.

I am not very clever.

2 I am a:

____

I have a snout.

I hunt for Rebel Birds.

I am sneaky.

3 I am a:

____

I have lots of weapons.

I have red eyes.

I can change shape.

4 I am a:

____

Find the **answers** on page 97.

Jabba the Hog

Complete the picture

Jabba the Hog is the meanest, fattest, most disgusting crime boss in the whole galaxy. He'll eat anything that isn't nailed down (and some things that are). One thing is for certain, you don't want to get anywhere near this big glob of grease!

Read about Chuck and Stella's run-in with Jabba, then draw Jabba into the picture to complete it.

Frozen!

Lard Vader has had poor Chuck frozen in carbonite! He was just testing the machine to see if it could freeze Red Skywalker. He doesn't need Chuck, so he sells him to Jabba the Hog.

Stella to the rescue

Stella uses a clever disguise to sneak into Jabba's dark, creepy palace on Tatooine. She defrosts Chuck, and they are about to escape when they are disturbed...

Caught in the act

The door behind them opens to reveal big, fat, slimy Jabba. Chuck and Stella are captured and chained up in his throne room. Only Red can save them now!

Add some of Jabba's **drool** to your picture.

What colour are Jabba's **eyes**?

Draw and Learn

Colour in Jabba's **green, slimy** skin.

Describe Jabba the Hog here.

Factivity Challenge

Test your knowledge on Chapter 2

Answer each question. If you need help, look back through the section.

Now that you have finished the second chapter of the book, take the Factivity Challenge to find out if you know the Pig Empire's secrets.

1. Find the sticker that best matches the description:

This crazy Sith Pig uses a double-bladed lightsaber

2. Which one of these is a Sith Pig?

Darth Spatula ☐ **Darth Porker** ☐ **Darth Swindle** ☐

3. Lard Vader used to be a Jedi Bird.

True ☐ **False** ☐

4. What kind of pig is this? ______________________

____

5. The Sith Pig with a white beard is Count ______________________.

Find the **answers** on page 97.

Now that you have finished the Challenge, fill this scene with your extra stickers!

Chapter 3

Awesome Vehicles

The galaxy is big. Birds and pigs both need vehicles to get around, and to battle each other. The Rebels may have style on their side, but the Pig Empire's mighty (and seriously ugly) war machines threaten to ruffle their feathers!

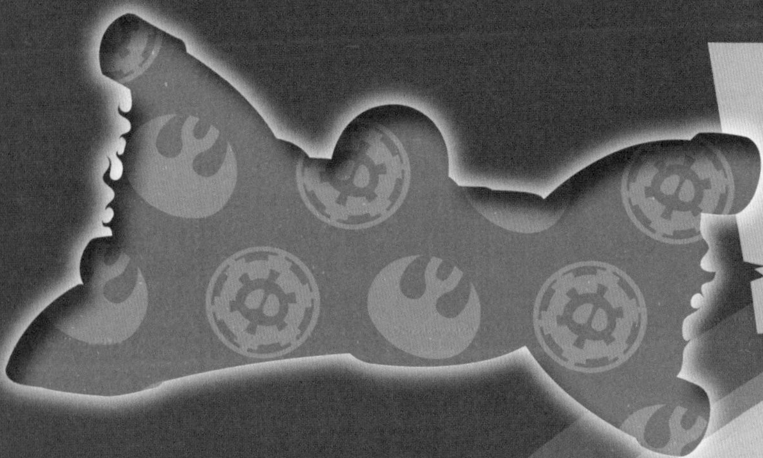

Birdfighter

Rebel Birdfighters can fly rings around the Pig Empire's TIE fighters. With an angry pilot behind the controls, you wouldn't want to get in its way!

Star Destroyer

Big, fast, triangular – Pig Empire Star Destroyers are all of these things. There aren't many things that can scare a Rebel Bird, but Star Destroyers are one!

Mighty Falcon

Chuck "Ham" Solo's *Mighty Falcon* might not look like much, but she's the fastest hunk of junk in the galaxy!

Find the **stickers** at the back of the book.

TIE fighter

TIE fighters are the Pig Empire's standard starfighter. They are not very advanced, but they are cheap, which means more money left over to spend on junk food.

Jabba's sail barge

Any self-respecting crime boss needs a stylish mode of transportation. Jabba the Hog uses his sail barge to roam the sandy wastes of Tattooine, searching for food to steal and eat.

AT-AT

Unlike the Rebel Birds, the Pork side is all about brawn instead of brains. The AT-AT is built to crush enemies under its giant metal trotters.

Speeder bike

High speeds and a lack of opposable thumbs shouldn't mix, but that doesn't seem to stop the pigs jumping on these lightning-quick speeder bikes.

Naboo cruiser

This sleak vessel is Queen Peckmé Amidala's personal starship. It doesn't have any weapons, but it makes up for it with speed and style.

Plucky Pilots

Match the pilot to their vehicle

The galaxy is full of daring pilots who love getting behind the controls of mobile machines. Some pilots want to explore space, while others like to zoom across planets. Either way, their favourite vehicle usually matches their personality.

Read about the different vehicles, then decide who pilots each one.

AT-AT

AT-ATs are big, slow, nearly impossible to destroy and carry more weapons than is sensible. They are the Pig Empire's chunkiest weapon.

Naboo cruiser

This ship was built for the Queen of Naboo. Since it was made for royalty, it has stylish design, and a comfortable (but classy) interior.

Sail barge

This unusual ship's massive pilot loves junk food so much, he will travel across his planet's vast deserts just to pig out on some!

Speeder bike

Speeder bikes are lightning fast. Unfortunately pigs aren't known for their quick reflexes, and fiery crashes are common.

Fear of flying

Flying through space isn't easy. There are asteroids, black holes, gamma ray bursts and red giants to watch out for. If you want to survive as a pilot, you will need nerves of steel, lightning-quick reflexes and a healthy dose of good luck!

Find the **stickers** at the back of the book.

Fact Challenge

Pilot #1

This pilot has a need for speed. His vehicle is so fast, if he ever fell off he would probably end up as bacon bits.

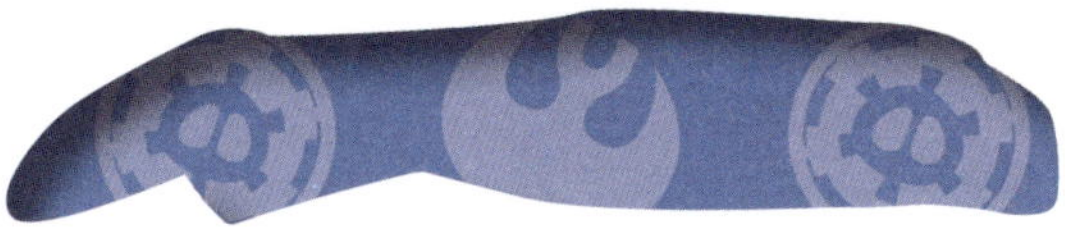

1 I pilot the ____________

Pilot #2

There aren't many vehicles big and strong enough to transport this lump of lard. He uses his unusual craft to travel across the sandy deserts of Tatooine.

2 I pilot the ____________

Pilot #3

This pilot prefers to drive slowly, rather than zooming off to places. His vehicle has thick armour so he doesn't worry about Rebel Bird attacks.

3 I pilot the ____________

Pilot #4

This pilot is quite fussy when it comes to long-distance travel. Only a comfortable, stylish craft will do.

4 I pilot the ____________

X-wing Birdfighters

Complete the sticker jigsaw

Rebel Birds zoom into battle in sleek X-wing Birdfighters. Pig Empire TIE fighters are just flying targets for these mean, supreme fighting machines!

Read about the X-wing Birdfighter, then use the stickers of the Birdfighter pieces to put it together.

R2-EGG2

Flying through space is really hard. Even the best pilot birds need a droid co-pilot to help them out!

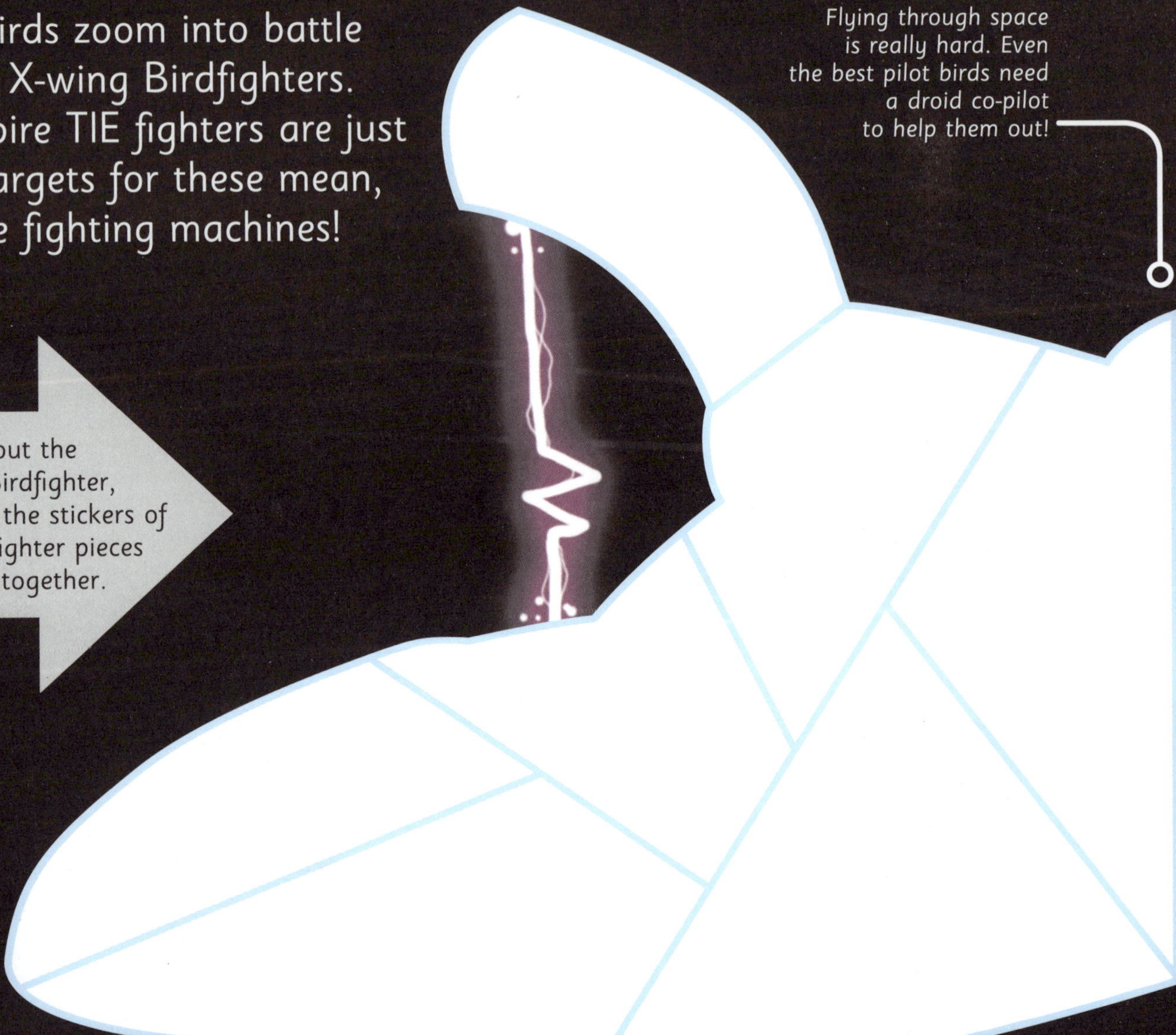

Beak nose cone

The nose cone at the front of the ship holds important sensors. It is painted like a big beak to scare the bacon out of pig pilots!

Blue Squadron

The fearless fliers of Blue Squadron always attack in threes. They are ace pilots, sworn to defeat the nasty Pig Empire, and their stylish blue helmets are famous across the galaxy!

Shipshape

The Birdfighter is very cleverly designed. It is long and thin, which makes it difficult for TIE fighters to hit.

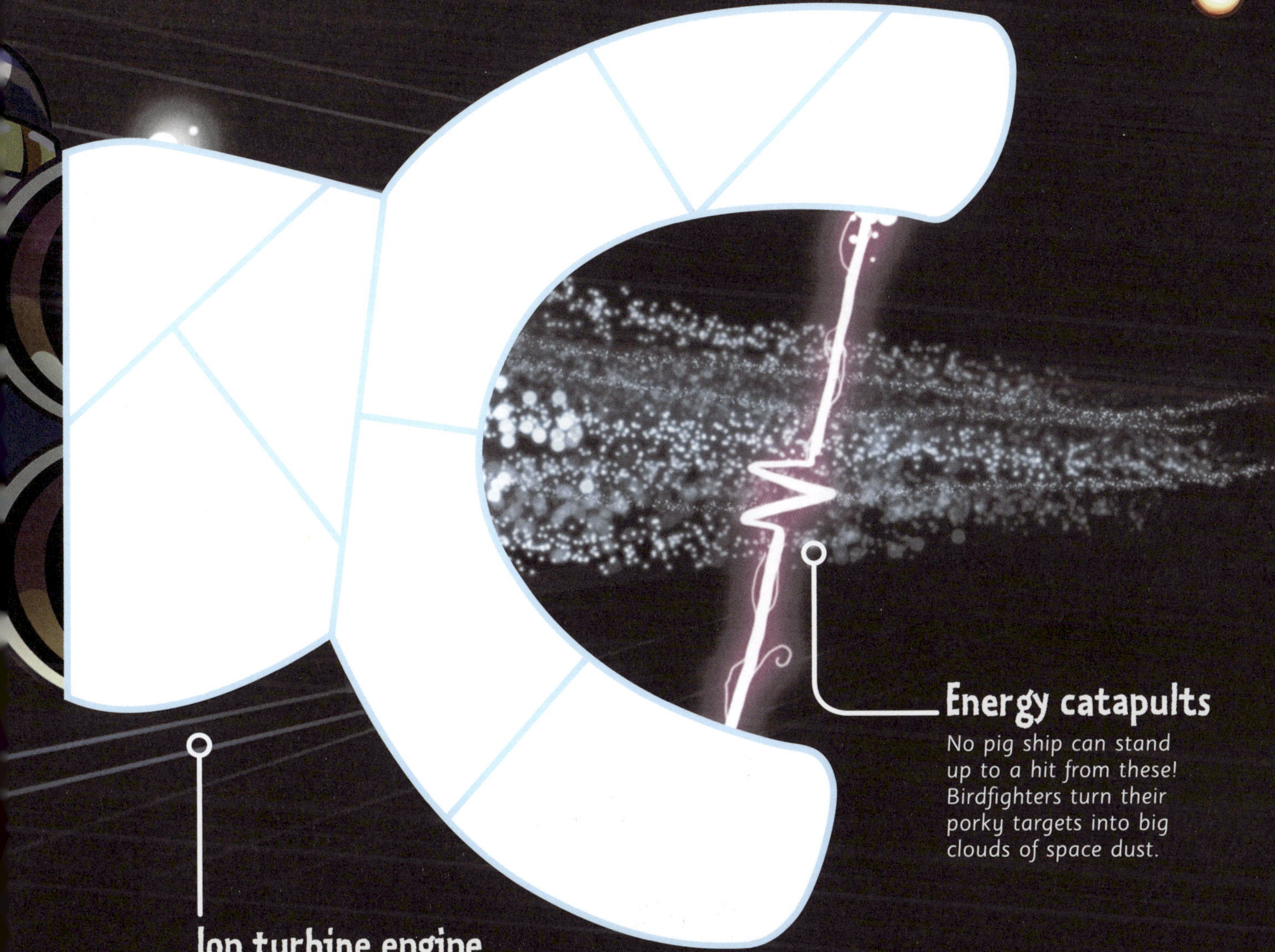

Energy catapults

No pig ship can stand up to a hit from these! Birdfighters turn their porky targets into big clouds of space dust.

Ion turbine engine

Rebel Birds like to go fast. These powerful engines help them charge towards their piggish foes.

TIE Fighters

Design your own fighter

Learn about pig TIE fighters, then design a new one of your own.

These vicious vehicles are the heart of the Pig Empire's space fleet. TIE (Twin Ion Engine) fighters might look sleek and sinister, but TIE fighter pilots aren't the cleverest pigs in the galaxy, so the Pig Empire mostly uses them as cannon fodder.

Standard TIE fighter

TIE fighters are fast, but they have no life-support systems or shields, which means that TIE missions tend to be short, and usually end with a fiery explosion.

Solar wing

TIE fighter engines are really simple – the wings gather in solar energy, and then the engines fire it out of the back!

Snout sensors

As well as looking cool, the TIE fighter's piggish snout holds sensors to sniff out rowdy Rebel Birds.

Piggy pilots

Only the most dedicated (and stupid) pigs become TIE fighter pilots – they usually don't last very long! TIE pilots have to wear special space suits so they can breathe in space.

Lard Vader

Back when he was a Jedi Bird, Lard Vader was a brave and skilful pilot. Now that he has turned to the Pork Side, he uses his skills to blow up Rebel Birds!

Lard Vader's TIE fighter

Lard Vader's personal advanced TIE fighter has been customised with bigger engines, bigger guns and a bigger fridge!

Custom cockpit

Lard Vader has had his ship modified to look like him, so he can terrify enemies over long distances.

Advanced wings

Lard Vader's ship is bigger than a standard TIE fighter, so it needs larger, more advanced wings to power its engines.

Remember to give your TIE fighter a **cockpit** in the **middle**!

Will your TIE fighter be **colourful** or **grey**?

What **shape** are the **wings** going to be?

This TIE fighter is a ______________________

Make sure you give your TIE fighter a **name**!

Captain's Journal

Help write Chuck's journal

The *Mighty Falcon* may be a shabby-looking starship, but the Bird Rebels never stop clucking about its adventures! The famous *Falcon* is full of souped-up technology, secret gadgets and weapons – it's the perfect vehicle to deal with the big pig problem head-on!

Slingshot style

A giant slingshot is a useful tool for starships that need a quick take-off. On Tatooine, this super stretchy one propels the *Mighty Falcon* into the sky. One bounce, and it soars away on its boosters.

Read all about Chuck's adventures on the *Mighty Falcon*, then fill in his journal.

Piggy parking

Not even the *Mighty Falcon* can resist the Pig Star's tractor beam! This invisible force sucks enemy ships into the Pig Star's landing bays, where Pigtroopers search the vehicle for foes. Yikes!

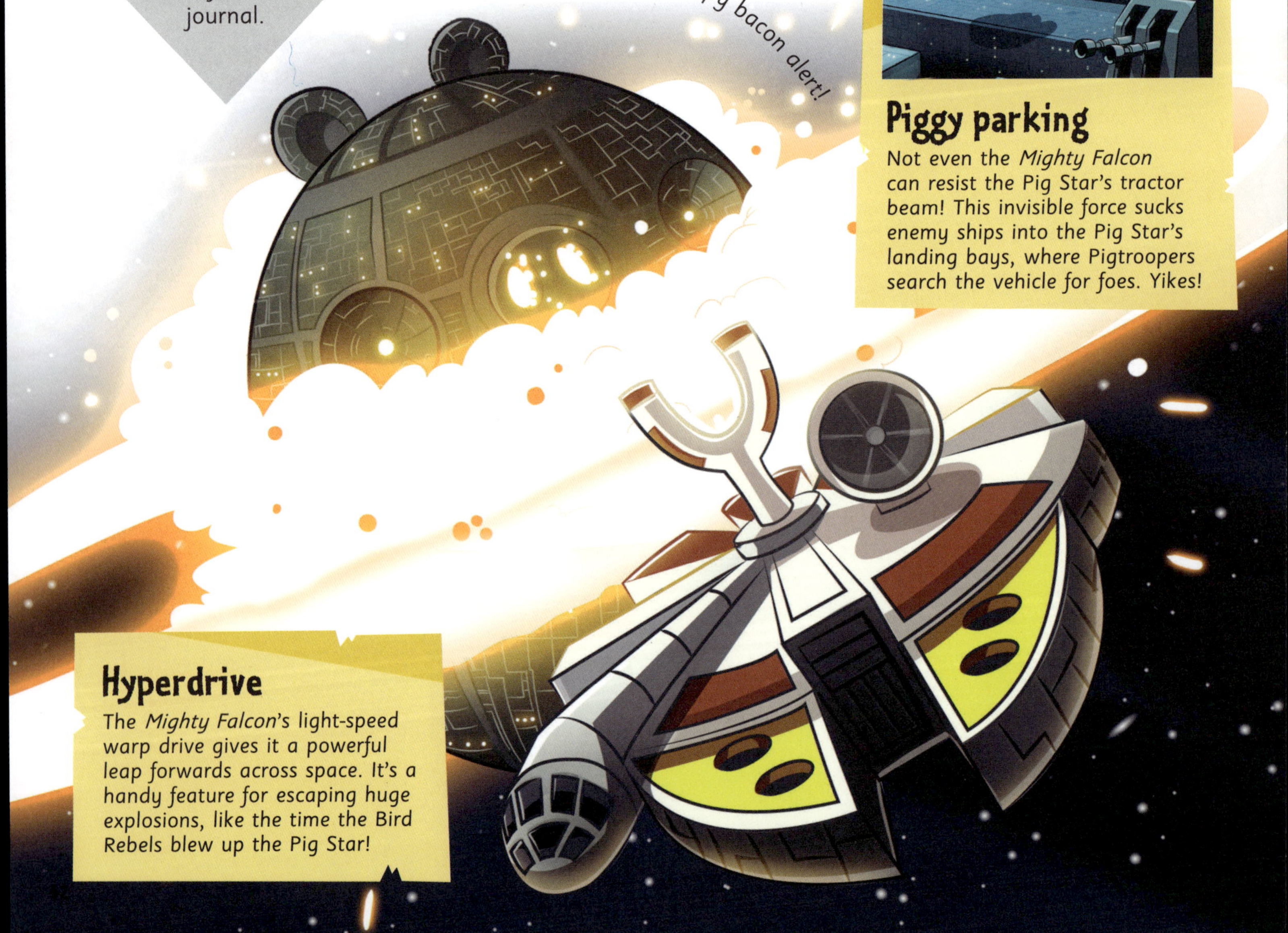

The Pig Star exploding – crispy bacon alert!

Hyperdrive

The *Mighty Falcon*'s light-speed warp drive gives it a powerful leap forwards across space. It's a handy feature for escaping huge explosions, like the time the Bird Rebels blew up the Pig Star!

Ship's captain

The *Mighty Falcon* is the pride and joy of its captain, Chuck. He won it in a bet from Lando Birdissian and he's never giving it back – ever! Co-pilot Terebacca is Chuck's faithful wingman in their space journeys.

MIGHTY FALCON JOURNAL

Location: Bouncing around on Tatooine

____

____

____

____

Location: Stuck in the Pig Star's tractor beam

____

____

____

____

Location: Flying away from the Pig Star – fast!

____

____

____

____

Use the information on the **opposite** page to help you **describe** the **action**.

Fact Challenge

How does the *Mighty Falcon* use its **technology** on journeys?

Finish Chuck's **entries** by **writing** about the *Mighty Falcon*'s **adventures**.

Star Destroyer

Color in the space battle

The fearsome fleet of the Pig Empire patrols the galaxy, snatching Rebel Birds wherever they find them. The Empire has many types of ships, but the most feared of all are the sinister Star Destroyers.

Learn about these starships, then colour in the picture opposite.

Star Destroyer

Star Destroyers are the Pig Empire's mightiest starships. These massive vessels are too strong to fight against, and too fast to escape from!

Tantive IV

The *Tantive IV* is Princess Stella Organa's personal starship. Its high speed and small size mean it can usually escape the Pork Side's clutches, but not this time!

You could add some **stars** or **planets** to the background.

Try to match the colours of the **ships** to the **pictures**.

Make sure you colour in the **explosions**.

What colour will the **planet** be?

Space Race

Race to Cloud City

Bounty hunters are searching space, trying to track down Rebel Birds for the pigs. The reward? Huge piles of candy! Runaway birds are rumored to be roosting on Cloud City. Bounty hunters across the galaxy race to get there!

Read the instructions to begin the mission.

The mission:

1. Grab something to use as a counter, and place it at the start.
2. Ask a friend to play and decide who will go first.
3. Take turns to roll a die, then move the number of spaces it shows.
4. Be the first bounty hunter to reach Cloud City.
5. Watch out for other vehicles and bounty hunters along the way!

Climb aboard!

Board your ship and head toward Cloud City. Fellow bounty hunter Boba Fatt pilots the *Slave I* starship. It may not look deadly, but inside its hull lie some scary hidden weapons, like a cannon, missiles, and a strong tractor beam. It's enough to put Jabba the Hog off his dinner!

Bounty hunters Zam Weasel and Greedork have their piggy peepers on the candy reward, too. You must find the birds first! Fly forward four spaces.

Start

1

2

3

4

5

18

19

20

21

TIE fighters form a higgledy-piggledy line to block off ships from your path. Speed forward one space.

The Bird Rebel Alliance's swift *Tantive IV* is more than a match for your *Slave I*. It is best to stay out of sight! Fly backward two spaces.

End

You've reached Cloud City!

Your destination, Cloud City, is surrounded by giant clouds. It floats in the atmosphere of the planet Bespin. Its high-tech security detects unidentified ships before they land in the docking bays, but your ship is too clever. Go get those birds!

Duck! R2-EGG2 and C-3PYOLK whizz through space in an escape pod at full velocity. Miss a turn while you keep away from the emergency shuttle's path.

Oh no – a flock of Mynhogs are on the loose! These pesky little parasites suck energy out of spaceships and drain their power. Miss a turn while you repair your ship.

It's the *Mighty Falcon*! You will win a record heap of candy if you get this famous ship! Move forward three spaces.

Surprise! Red appears in his super agile X-Wing Birdfighter. You must fly away as quickly as you can! Zoom backward two spaces.

Factivity Challenge

Test your knowledge on Chapter 3

Answer each question. If you need help, look back through the section.

Now that you have finished the third chapter of the book, take the Factivity Challenge to see if you have what it takes to be a pilot!

1. Find the sticker that best matches the description:

This ship is the Pig Empire's standard starfighter.

2. Which one of these is a Rebel Bird ship?

J-wing Birdfighter ☐ **X-wing Birdfighter** ☐ **F-wing Birdfighter** ☐

3. The *Tantive IV* is Lard Vader's personal starship.

True ☐ **False** ☐

4. Who pilots this ship? ____________________

____

5. Chuck "Ham" Solo pilots the ____________________.

Find the **answers** on page 97.

Now that you have finished the Challenge, fill this scene with your extra stickers!

Chapter 4

Galactic Battles

Space is not a peaceful place – the birds and pigs just can't seem to get along. On planets big and small, hot and cold, crazy conflicts rage for control of the galaxy, The Egg and any food that happens to be nearby.

The Battle of Naboo

The peaceful planet of Naboo has been invaded by the evil Pork Federation! Fearless Jedi Birds Quail-Gon and Obi-Wan Kaboomi must defeat an army of robotic battle pigs.

Lightsaber duels

Jedi Birds and Sith Pigs have used lightsabers to battle each other for thousands of years. For some reason, they think whacking each other with laser swords is more civilised than blasting each other.

Find the **stickers** at the back of the book.

Red and Vader

Red Skywalker knows that behind the armoured snout, there is still a Jedi Bird inside Lard Vader. If Red is to save him, first he must defeat him...

Weapons

You can't have a battle without any weapons. The galaxy is full of them! Some go "whoosh," while others go "fizz", "bang", "buzz" or "kapow!"

C-3PYOLK

C-3PYOLK was built many years ago, and since then has traveled from one side of the galaxy to the other. He is fluent in thousands of languages, so he makes the perfect travel partner!

The Battle of Hoth

The Pig Empire has sniffed out the Rebel Bird base on the icy planet of Hoth. The weather outside is frightful, but the pigs' AT-AT walkers are even worse!

Guide to the Galaxy

Complete C-3PYOLK's guide

I am C-3PYOLK, and I would like to welcome you to this great galaxy! There is so much to see and do here. You will need a guide to navigate this huge place. Being a helpful droid, I have started making one. You're welcome!

C-3PYOLK

C-3PYOLK is a friendly servant droid, and unlike the birds, he is never angry. He's actually a bit of a chicken!

Read about the planets, then complete C-3PYOLK's tourist guide.

Tatooine

Visit this planet at your peril! Tatooine is a scorching hot desert world that is sure to ruffle your feathers. Redkin Skywalker was hatched here, but don't tell the pigs!

Coruscant

Coruscant is so busy it makes me quite nervous! You have to be a night owl to perch here among the tall skyscrapers, as it is known as the city that never sleeps.

Dagobah

Watch out! This is one of the trickiest planets to land on. It is covered in smelly swamps and dark forests. Try to avoid its fearsome swamp creatures – if you can!

Hoth

Only a bird brain would visit the icy cold planet of Hoth! Spending even a few minutes on its snow-covered surface can freeze your delicate feathers.

Naboo

Beautiful Naboo has lush, grassy plains, warm weather, and stunning bird statues. You may even spot Naboo's wonderful Queen Peckmé flying about.

Tatooine

C-3PYOLK'S Guide to the Galaxy

1 ______ is a harsh desert planet, so it is scorching ______ here.

2 Coruscant is filled with lots of tall ______ This planet is very busy so don't expect to get any ______ at night.

3 The planet of ______ is covered with snow and ice.

Hoth

4 Naboo has lush grassy ______ , as well as a special royal resident named ______ .

5 ______ is a swampy planet. It is full of forests and fearsome ______ ______ .

Dagobah

Find the **answers** on page 97.

Wacky Weapons

Match the weapon to its user

Across the galaxy, birds and pigs fight each other using some pretty bizarre weaponry. Lightsabers, blasters and giant forks are all used in battle!

Work out which weapon belongs to each warrior, then place a sticker of their correct weapon next to them.

Yoda Bird

*He might be ancient and a bit absentminded, but in battle this **Jedi Bird** is no pushover! His glowing weapon gives him an edge over plump pigs.*

Jango Fatt

*As a **stylish** bounty hunter, Jango will only be seen with the coolest, shiniest, most up-to-date gadgets and weapons.*

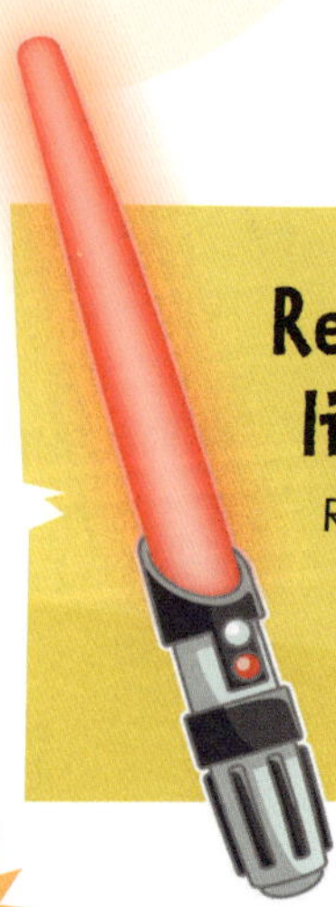

Red-bladed lightsaber

*Red is the colour of the **Pork Side**. Only a Sith Pig could use such a scary weapon.*

Blaster

*There is no match for a good blaster at a smuggler's side. A hit from this will knock any pig down to size, even at a **distance**.*

Green-bladed lightsaber

*Lightsabers are a civilised weapon from a less piggy age. This one's **colour** matches that of its **owner**.*

Chuck "Ham" Solo

As a daring **smuggler**, Chuck Solo thinks that lightsabers are too old-fashioned. He prefers to carry something with a bit more range.

Tusken Raider

These sinister swine come from the harsh deserts of the planet Tatooine. They lie in wait to ambush birds with their **pointy** weapons, and then steal their food.

Lard Vader

Lard Vader leads the Pig Empire into battle. Vader uses a weapon that only a **Sith Pig** would normally carry, but few know he was once a Jedi Bird!

Advanced blaster

A shiny blaster like this would only be used by someone with a strong sense of **style**.

Gaffi fork

This simple weapon is used by someone who likes to hide in the **desert,** and is always hungry.

Find the **stickers** at the back of the book.

Lightsaber Battle

Write in the speech bubbles

Quail-Gon, Darth Moar, and Obi-Wan are locked in a fierce lightsaber duel. Who will be victorious: the Jedi Birds or the Sith Pig? It's two against one, but Darth Moar is a powerful warrior who is not afraid of fighting dirty.

Lightsaber skills

It takes great coordination, courage and a strong wing or trotter to wield these plasma-powered blades. That's why lazy Lard Vader makes the Pigtroopers lug his around for him when he's not using it!

Read the comic strip and write the speech bubbles.

You could write in **pencil** first, and then use a **pen**.

What could **Quail-Gon** be shouting at **Darth Moar**?

What sort of noise could **Quail-Gon** be making here?

What is **Obi-Wan** thinking here?

Fact Challenge

The Battle of Hoth

Find the stickers

Lard Vader and his swine minions have sniffed out the Rebel Birds' hidden base on the planet Hoth. Vader sends in his best snow vehicles to destroy the bird base. The Rebel Birds need to escape the Pig Empire's stomping trotters, and fast!

Read about the Battle of Hoth, then use stickers to fill in the missing parts of the scene.

Icy base

Hoth looks like a giant snowball. Its freezing temperatures and snowy, icy landscape mean that few are plucky enough to go there – apart from the Rebel Birds, that is.

Find the **stickers** at the back of the book.

AT-AT

AT-ATs are perfectly suited to battles on ice. The big trotters make them very stable, and their big guns make the Rebel Birds fly for cover!

AT-AT pilot

It takes a special kind of pilot to drive a giant mechanical pig. They need a head for heights and a love of blowing things up.

AT-ST

AT-STs are smaller and faster than AT-ATs. They don't have as many weapons, but they can trample even the quickest Rebel Birds.

AT-ST pilot

AT-ST pilots are daredevils. They wear less armour than their AT-AT pilot friends, as getting a good view of the battle is more important to them.

Red vs Lard Vader

Complete the comic strip

The battle between Rebel Birds and Sith Lards for The Egg leads to one final fight. Lard Vader and Red Skywalker may be father and son, but that won't stop them from going against each other – or will it?

Read the comic strip about the deadly duel and colour in the final picture.

Lard Vader can't bear to kill his son, but Red is able to strike Darth Swindle! As the evil pig falls, he zaps Lard Vader with his Force lightning.

Red is sad to lose his father, but he is happy that the Rebel Birds have won. Now that the powerful porkers have been defeated, the galaxy is finally safe!

Lard Vader asks Red to take his helmet off so he can look at Red with his own eyes. Red realises there is still a good bird hidden beneath Lard Vader's piggy helmet.

What does Lard Vader look like under his helmet?

Battle of Naboo

Draw your own pig army

Battle pigs are robotic hogs that have just one brain between them. The dumb droids are usually unsuccessful in battle, but somehow they manage to overpower the Jedi Birds on Naboo.

Read about the Battle of Naboo and the battle pigs. Then design your own battle pigs for a pig army.

Fight or flight?

Quail-Gon and Obi-Wan find themselves in a sticky situation in a Pork Federation control ship after being tricked. The plucky birds are soon confronted by an airheaded army of battle pigs.

Naboo invasion

The Jedi escape to Naboo, but the battle pigs follow them and invade the planet. Obi-Wan and Quail-Gon put up a good fight, but are soon outnumbered by the half-witted hogs!

Battle pig

The battle pigs are rarely seen alone. They prefer to stick together in a porky pack. They have a vocoder voicebox in their snouts and spend all their time moaning.

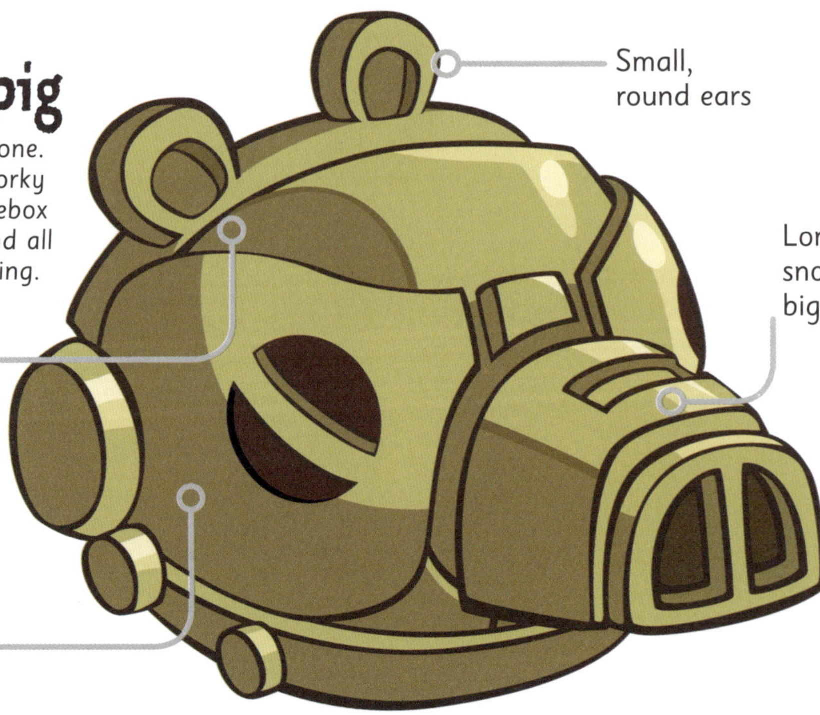

Your pig army should **surround** Obi-Wan and Quail-Gon.

What sort of **snout** will your battle pigs have?

Your pig army could be any **colour**.

Don't forget to draw **ears** on your pig soldiers.

Factivity Challenge

Test your knowledge on Chapter 4

Answer each question. If you need help, look back through the section.

Now that you have finished the fourth chapter of the book, take the Factivity Challenge to see if you know your way around the galaxy.

1. Find the sticker that best matches the description:

This planet is covered in smelly swamps and dark forests.

2. Which two of these are famous battles?

The Battle of Didgeridoo ☐ **The Battle of Naboo** ☐ **The Battle of Hoth** ☐

3. Darth Moar defeats Quail-Gon in a lightsaber duel.

True ☐ **False** ☐

4. What is this vehicle? ____________________

5. The planet Naboo is invaded by an army of ____________________.

Find the **answers** on page 97.